What Are We Fighting For?

Coming Together Around What Matters Most

Leader Guide

What Are We Fighting For?
Coming Together Around
What Matters Most

What Are We Fighting For?
Coming Together Around What Matters Most
978-1-5018-1505-8
978-1-5018-1506-5 *eBook*

What Are We Fighting For? Leader Guide
978-1-5018-1507-2
978-1-5018-1508-9 *eBook*

What Are We Fighting For? DVD
9781501815119

Coming Together Around What Matters Most:
A Six-Week Devotional Journey
978-1-5018-1509-6
978-1-5018-1510-2 *eBook*

What Are We Fighting For? Pastor Resources Download
978-1-5018-1513-3

For more information, visit www.AbingdonPress.com.

Thomas J. Bickerton

WHAT ARE WE
FIGHTING FOR?

LEADER GUIDE
by Barbara Dick

COMING TOGETHER AROUND
WHAT MATTERS MOST

Abingdon Press / Nashville

What Are We Fighting For?
Coming Together Around What Matters Most—
Leader Guide

This book is printed on elemental, chlorine-free paper.
ISBN 978-1-5018-1507-2

16 17 18 19 20 21 22 23 24 25 — 10 9 8 7 6 5 4 3 2 1
MANUFACTURED IN THE UNITED STATES OF AMERICA

CONTENTS

To the Leader 7

Session 1: Getting to the Heart of the Matter 13

Session 2: Three Reminders for the Journey 19

Session 3: Discerning What Matters Most 25

Session 4: Filling in the Blank with the Essentials 33

Session 5: Paddling in the Same Canoe 41

Session 6: Finishing with Love 49

Handouts 56

TO THE LEADER

With all the issues facing The United Methodist Church today, there are plenty of theories and opinions about what we should do. Many are weary of the relentless bickering associated with all the rhetoric, wondering, *what are we fighting for?* This question not only points us to the futility of our disunity but also compels us to consider what we are fighting *for*—what deserves our greatest intensity and effort as we seek to be faithful followers of Jesus Christ.

In this study, Bishop Thomas J. Bickerton offers a way to move beyond all the discord to a hope-filled future, inviting us to shift our attention from issues we fight *about* to the essentials that are worth fighting *for* so that the gospel of Jesus Christ becomes a vibrant part of our lives and witness. As group leader, you will lead others in a process of discernment that will help you come together around what matters most and become a relevant and vital presence in the community and world. This process is dependent on the presence and guidance of the Holy Spirit. Scripture tells us that where two or three are gathered together, we can be assured of the presence of the Holy Spirit, working in and through all those gathered. As you prepare to lead, pray for that presence and expect that you will experience it.

This six-session study makes use of the following components:

- the book *What Are We Fighting For?* by Thomas J. Bickerton
- this Leader Guide
- the video segments on the companion DVD
- a book of daily devotions, as well as downloadable pastor resources for leading a congregational focus

In addition to the study book, group members will also need Bibles and either a notebook or electronic tablet for journaling. Be sure to notify those interested in the study in advance so that they may obtain copies of the book and read the Introduction and Chapter 1 before the first session.

Using This Guide with Your Group

Because no two groups are alike, this guide is structured to give you flexibility and choice in tailoring the sessions for your group. The basic session format is designed for a 50-minute Sunday school or other small group session, with an extended format option of 80 minutes for those groups desiring more time for deeper discernment. Suggested time allotments are provided only as a general guide. Select ahead of time which activities and discussion questions your group will do, for how long, and in what order—adapting the material as you wish to meet the schedule and needs of your particular group. Depending on which activities you select, special preparation may be necessary. Instructions regarding preparation are provided at the beginning of each session plan. (*Note:* The handouts provided at the back of this book are intended to serve as a preview. For 8 ½ x 11 printable PDFs, go to Abingdonpress.com/WhatAreWeFightingFor.)

Basic Session Format
50 minutes (*Extended Format Option: 80 minutes)

Planning the Session (In Advance)
Session Goals
Biblical Foundation
Special Preparation

Getting Started
Welcome and Opening Prayer (3 minutes)

Connecting the Dots
Video (15 minutes)
Biblical Foundation (5 minutes)
Book Study (20 minutes)
*For Deeper Discernment (Additional 30 minutes—Extended Format Only)

The Way Forward
Practical Exercises and Reflections for the Week (5 minutes)
Closing Prayer (2 minutes)

Whether using the basic or extended format, two primary objectives undergird each group session: 1) in Connecting the Dots, participants will find help for connecting their beliefs with practice; 2) in The Way Forward, group members will discover tangible ways they can implement what they've discovered in their daily lives as well as in the life of the congregation.

As your group comes together around what matters most and discerns the ways your congregation can implement those essentials as you pursue the call to make disciples, you will foster a spirit of unity and create a contagious climate of renewal. Our hope and prayer is that together you will find the courage to say yes to the things that are worth fighting for and no to the fighting that so easily weighs us down and distracts us.

Helpful Hints

Before you get started, here are a few helpful hints to equip you for preparing, shaping, and managing the group experience:

Preparing for the Session

- Pray for the leading of the Holy Spirit as you prepare for the study. Pray for discernment for yourself and for each member of the study group.
- Before each session, read the book chapter and familiarize yourself with the content.
- Choose the session elements you will use during the group session, including the specific discussion questions you plan to cover. Be prepared, however, to adjust the session as group members interact and as questions arise. Prepare carefully, but allow space for the Holy Spirit to move in and through the group members and through you as facilitator.
- If you plan to use video clips or music suggestions, obtain appropriate projection equipment and test it before the session in which you plan to use it.
- Prepare the space where the group will meet so that the environment will enhance the learning process. Ideally, group members should be seated around a table or in a circle so that all can see one another. Moveable chairs are best, because the group will often form pairs or small groups for discussion.
- Bring a supply of Bibles for those who forget to bring their own. Provide a variety of translations.
- For most sessions you will also need an easel with paper and markers, a whiteboard and markers, or some other means of posting group questions and responses.

Shaping the Learning Environment

- Begin and end on time.
- Establish a welcoming space. Consider the room temperature, access to amenities, hospitality, outside noise, and privacy. Consider using a small cross or candle as a focal point for times of prayer.
- Create a climate of openness, encouraging group members to participate as they feel comfortable. Some participants may be uncomfortable or embarrassed about sharing their experiences. Be on the lookout for signs of discomfort in those who may be silent, and encourage them to express their thoughts and feelings honestly. Assure the group members that passing on a question is always acceptable.
- Remember that some people will jump right in with answers and comments, while others need time to process what is being discussed.
- If you notice that some group members seem never to be able to enter the conversation, ask them if they have thoughts to share. Give everyone a chance to talk, but keep the conversation moving. Moderate to prevent a few individuals from doing all the talking.
- Make use of the exercises that invite sharing in pairs. Those who are reluctant to speak out in a group setting may be more comfortable sharing one-on-one and reporting back to the group. This can often be an effective means of helping people grow more comfortable sharing in the larger setting. It also helps to avoid the dominance of the group by one or two participants (including you!).
- If no one answers at first during discussions, do not be afraid of silence. Help the group become comfortable with waiting. If no one responds, try reframing the language of the question. If no responses are forthcoming, venture an answer yourself and ask for comments.

- Model openness as you share with the group. Group members will follow your example. If you limit your sharing to a surface level, others will follow suit.
- Encourage multiple answers or responses before moving on.
- Ask, "Why?" or "Why do you believe that?" or "Can you say more about that?" to help continue a discussion and give it greater depth.
- Affirm others' responses with comments such as "great" or "thanks" or "good insight"—especially if it's the first time someone has spoken during the group session.
- Monitor your own contributions. If you are doing most of the talking, back off so that you do not train the group to listen rather than speak up.
- Remember that you do not have all the answers. Your job is to keep the discussion going and encourage participation.

Managing the Session
- Honor the time schedule. If a session is running longer than expected, get consensus from the group before continuing beyond the agreed-upon ending time.
- When someone arrives late or must leave early, pause the session briefly to welcome them or bid them farewell. Changes in the makeup of the group change the dynamics of the discussion and need to be acknowledged. Every group member is important to the entire group.
- Involve group members in various aspects of the group session, such as saying prayers or reading the Scripture.
- As always in discussions that may involve personal sharing, confidentiality is essential. Group members should never pass along stories that have been shared in the group. Remind the group members at each session: confidentiality is crucial to the success of this study.

Session 1

GETTING TO THE HEART OF THE MATTER

Planning the Session

Session Goals

As a result of conversations and activities connected with this session, group members should begin to:

- Consider the eternal nature of our relationship with God.
- Understand the role of the five I's—inspiration, integration, isolation, independence, and invitation—in the vitality of the faith community.
- Explore the relationship of their individual stories with the larger story of faith.

Biblical Foundation

> So we're not giving up. How could we! Even though on
> the outside it often looks like things are falling apart on
> us, on the inside, where God is making new life, not
> a day goes by without his unfolding grace. These hard
> times are small potatoes compared to the coming good
> times, the lavish celebration prepared for us. There's far
> more here than meets the eye. The things we see now
> are here today, gone tomorrow. But the things we can't
> see now will last forever.
>
> (2 Corinthians 4:16-18 *The Message*)

Special Preparation

- In advance of the first session, ask participants to bring
  either a notebook or an electronic means of journaling,
  such as a tablet, to each group session. Provide writing
  paper and pens for those who may need them. Also have
  Bibles available for those who do not bring one.
- Make sure all participants have a copy of the book *What
  Are We Fighting For?* Invite them to read the Introduction
  and Chapter 1 in advance of the first session.
- Have available large sheets of blank paper (newsprint)
  or construction paper and colored markers for group
  activity.
- Make copies of Handout 1: The Roots of Our Faith for the
  group (see page 56 for a preview; for a printable PDF, see
  Abingdonpress.com/WhatAreWeFightingFor).
- As leader, go over the session in advance and select or adapt
  the activities you think will work best for your group in the
  time allotted. Consider your own responses to questions
  you will pose to the group.
- Make nametags available if desired.

Getting Started

Welcome and Opening Prayer (3 minutes)

As participants arrive, welcome them to the study and invite them to make use of one of the available Bibles, if they did not bring one. Offer the following prayer, pray one of your own, or invite a group member to pray.

Gracious and loving God, as we begin this study, open us to your presence and fill us—our time, our conversations, our reflections, our doubts, and our fears—with the joy of exploration and the wisdom of your love. We gather together in Jesus' name. Amen.

Connecting the Dots

Video (15 minutes)

Play the video for Session 1. This segment suggests that the problem in the church today is a spiritual issue. We have relied too much on our own solutions and not enough on the presence of God to inform, bless, and equip us for the journey that is before us. We are encouraged to push off and let go, which means finding the faith once again to trust in the power of God's presence to safely guide us back to solid ground. With God's help, a calming presence of assurance is possible.

Choose from the following for a brief discussion:

- Do you agree that the problem we face in the church today is largely a spiritual issue? Why or why not? If you agree, how would you describe this spiritual problem?
- In what ways are we, the church, stuck on the side of a cliff? What emotions and anxieties is this producing, and how is this affecting our public witness?

- What would it mean for us to "push off and let go," relying on God's direction rather than our own efforts? How willing are we to put our opinions aside for a while and put our lives into the hands of the One who can see us through?

Biblical Foundation (5 minutes)

The book's introduction ends with a quotation from 2 Corinthians 4:16-18 as interpreted in *The Message*. Read the passage aloud and discuss:

- What does the passage teach about our relationship with God? About faith?

Book Study (20 minutes)

Chapter 1 of the book begins with a story about a bishop identifying an issue as a "spiritual problem" rather than a problem of "morale." Invite a volunteer to read the opening paragraphs of Chapter 1. Ask the group members to share the ways they see the difficulties facing the church—both the local congregation and the larger connection—as being rooted in a spiritual problem.

Explore the chapter's content together with the following exercise:

The Five I's

The author explores five aspects of community life—inspiration, integration, isolation, independence, invitation—that help us understand the root cause of our spiritual problem.

Break the group into five small groups (or pairs, depending on the size of the group) and assign one "I" to each group. Each group will explore these questions:

- How does the author define this "I"?
- In what ways does this "I" help us understand our relationship with God?

- Where do we see this "I" expressed in our faith
  community? In the larger connection?

Ask the groups to record their responses on newsprint and choose a reporter. When the groups have completed their work, ask the reporter from each group to post the newsprint and share their findings.

Invite the entire group to share the ways in which the five "I's" can help us focus attention on our eternal relationship with God, rather than the day-to-day issues of the faith community.

For Deeper Discernment
(Additional 30 minutes—Extended Format Only)

Post the following questions on newsprint or whiteboard:

- When was the first time Jesus became more than just a
  name to you?
- When was the last time Jesus was more than just a name to you?

Invite participants into conversation in small groups of three or four. The questions are designed to help people think about how their relationship with God has evolved over time. This process helps us learn how to tell our faith stories and how to actively listen to and learn from the stories of others as all of our stories continue.

Give the small groups 15 minutes to share their responses with one another. Remind them that as each person shares, the task of the listeners is to attend to and receive the story in prayerful silence. Remind them that each person should have opportunity to share, and that persons may choose not to share.

At the end of the 15 minutes of small-group time, invite the groups back together. Ask them to share insights gained from hearing one another's stories and from sharing their own. How has their faith changed and grown over time? What do the variety of conversion stories tell us about the nature of God and our relationship with God and one another?

The Way Forward

Practical Exercises and Reflections for the Week (5 minutes)

Exercises in this section will build on one another as the sessions progress, much as a tree grows from the roots in the soil through the trunk, branches, and leaves. The practical exercises for this first session deal with the "heart of the matter," the roots of our faith.

Read this quotation from the book to the group: "I believe we are missing the one element key to the whole conversation: *the need for confession and a renewed desire to seek the heart of God*" (page 26). Invite group members to share their understanding of this statement and the ways it inspires and invites them to deeper faith.

Distribute copies of Handout 1: The Roots of Our Faith (see page 56 for a preview; for a printable PDF, see Abingdonpress.com/ WhatAreWeFightingFor). Instruct group members to post the handout somewhere they will see it daily, using it as a springboard for reflection and action in the coming week. They may think about the five "I" words throughout the week as they encounter conversations and activities in their personal lives and the life of your church, or they may prefer to focus on a different word each day. Encourage them to record their thoughts and experiences in their journals. You also might consider texting one word per day to all group members and inviting a daily response. Tell participants to be sure to bring their journals with them next time, when they will have the opportunity to share highlights with the group.

Closing Prayer (2 minutes)

God of eternal love, fill us with your power as we leave this place, so that all we have shared and learned here helps us to be more faithful disciples. As your church in and for the world, we pray in the name of Jesus the Christ. Amen.

Session 2

THREE REMINDERS
FOR THE JOURNEY

Planning the Session

Session Goals

As a result of conversations and activities connected with this session, group members should begin to:

- Understand what it means to lighten up in difficult situations.
- Learn the value of collaboration.
- Explore empathy, opening to see the view of others as valuable and self as a work in progress.
- Practice healthy relationship skills in their homes, work, and at church.

Biblical Foundation

"Are you as committed to me as I am to you?... If so, then give me your hand." (2 Kings 10:15 CEB)

"Is your heart as true to mine as mine is to yours?... If it is, give me your hand." (2 Kings 10:15 NRSV).

Special Preparation

- Ask participants to bring either a notebook or an electronic means of journaling, such as a tablet. Provide writing paper and pens for those who may need them. Also have Bibles available for those who do not bring one.
- Invite participants to read Chapter 2 in advance of the session and remind them to bring their journals with them.
- Make copies of Handout 2: The Soil of Relationships for the group (see page 57 for a preview; for a printable PDF, see Abingdonpress.com/WhatAreWeFightingFor).
- Have available large sheets of blank paper (newsprint) or construction paper and colored markers for group activity.
- As leader, you'll want to go over the session in advance and select or adapt the activities you think will work best for your group in the time allotted. Consider your own responses to questions you will pose to the group.
- Make nametags available if desired.

Getting Started

Welcome and Opening Prayer (3 minutes)

As participants arrive, welcome them to the study and invite them to make use of one of the available Bibles, if they did not bring one. Offer the following prayer, pray one of your own, or invite a group member to pray.

Joyous and giving God, we gather to learn, share, laugh, and grow in faith and joy. Accompany us on the journey. Amen.

Connecting the Dots

Video (15 minutes)

Play the video for Session 2. This segment encourages us to lighten up, loosen up, and have a little fun in order to create the right posture for the Spirit to help us determine what matters most. We are all works in progress, so we should remain open to what God has in store for us next. And we are encouraged to have a posture of faith, confident that God is able to do immeasurably more than we can imagine.

Choose from the following for a brief discussion:

- In what ways do you think we are too tight and stiff as a church? How might we reclaim the art of spontaneity and simplicity?
- How can we create the right posture for the Spirit to "get a hold of us"? Why is this critical to the process of determining what matters most?
- How can remembering that we are all works in progress help us keep ourselves open to what God has in store for us and also help us collaborate with others?

Biblical Foundation (5 minutes)

Read aloud 2 Kings 10:15 and discuss:

- What does the passage teach about human relationships? About our relationship with God?
- In what circumstances would it be difficult for you to offer this invitation? Why?

Book Study (20 minutes)

Invite group members to *briefly* share highlights in response to their focus on the five I's since the last session (Handout 1: The Roots of Our Faith). Remind the group that these I's are the roots of faith. Then point out that the three reminders of Chapter 2—to loosen up, to collaborate, and to be open to change—are the soil or ecosystem in which healthy relationships are planted.

Explore the chapter content together with the following exercises:

Empathy and Active Listening

Divide the group into pairs. Have one person in the pair choose a role from the list below (post the roles on newsprint or a whiteboard). For one minute, the partner will assume that role and explain why he or she behaves in that way. Then the other partner will assume a role from the list and share for one minute. The job of the listener is simply to hear and receive.

- Someone who interrupts and cuts others off when they speak.
- Someone who complains about the style of worship.
- Someone who goes on and on during prayer concerns.
- Someone who dominates the conversation.
- Someone who is consistently late for appointments and meetings.

After the pairs have had time to share, invite the group to talk about the experience of trying to justify behaviors they might not admire—walking in another's shoes—and the experience of receiving another's self-justification in silence. This exercise often evokes laughter as people recognize themselves or others they know. Acknowledge this as a healthy sign of our ability to lighten up. (This exercise was inspired by the work of Jorge Cherbosque, Lee Gardenswartz, and Anita Rowe, of the Emotional Intelligence and Diversity Institute, http://www.eidi-results.org/.)

Together We Can

Through the chapter's three reminders—loosen up, collaborate, be open to the possibility of change—the author teaches us that life in community is not about agreeing on everything; it is about caring enough to listen, opening our hearts and minds to hear, and bringing grace and joy into each encounter. Break the group into three small groups and assign one of the three reminders to each group. Have each group explore one or more of these questions (post them on newsprint or a whiteboard):

- What does the author teach about this reminder?
- What does this reminder teach us about God? About human beings?
- Where do we see this reminder expressed in our faith community? In the larger connection?

Ask each group to choose a reporter. When the groups have completed work, have the reporter from each group share their findings.

For Deeper Discernment
(Additional 30 minutes—Extended Format Only)

Post the following questions on newsprint or a whiteboard:

- What persons have been models or mentors in your life?
- How did they embody the three reminders?
- How might you become a mentor for someone else?

Invite participants to reflect on and perhaps write out responses to the questions. Then divide into small groups of three or four people to share responses and talk about the ways mentors and guides influence the way we live the life of faith. These conversations invite us to see the ways we learn from others about living with integrity, whether we are receiving or offering guidance.

Give the small groups 15 minutes to share their responses with one another. Remind them that as each person shares, the task of the listeners is to attend to and receive the story in prayerful silence. Remind them that each person should have an opportunity to share, and that persons may choose not to share.

At the end of the 15 minutes of small group time, invite the groups back together. Ask them to share insights gained from hearing one another's stories and from sharing their own. How have their faith and their relationships with God and others been influenced by the guides and mentors in their lives?

The Way Forward

Practical Exercises and Reflections for the Week (5 minutes)

Exercises in this section build on one another as the sessions progress, much as a tree grows from the roots in the soil through the trunk, branches, and leaves. This session's practical exercises deal with the quality of the soil in which we are planted—our relationships.

Distribute copies of Handout 2: The Soil of Healthy Relationships (see page 57 for a preview; for a printable PDF, see Abingdonpress .com/WhatAreWeFightingFor). Instruct group members to post the handout somewhere they will see it daily, using it as a springboard for reflection and action in the coming week. Invite participants to seek opportunities to listen with love and learn from others, and encourage them to record their thoughts and experiences in their journals. Tell them to be sure to bring their journals with them next time, when they will have the opportunity to share highlights with the group.

Closing Prayer (2 minutes)

God of transformation, God of joy, walk with us this week as we stretch to learn new skills in the ways we communicate and share with others. Amen.

Session 3

DISCERNING WHAT MATTERS MOST

Planning the Session

Session Goals

As a result of conversations and activities connected with this session, group members should begin to:

- Learn the five guidelines that build the spiritual practice of discernment.
- Explore the links between passion, belief, action, and God.
- Begin to discern nonessentials and essentials—what is worth fighting for.

Biblical Foundation

> And this is my prayer, that your love may overflow more and more with knowledge and full insight to help you to determine what is best, so that in the day of Christ you may be pure and blameless, having produced the harvest of righteousness that comes through Jesus Christ for the glory and praise of God. (Philippians 1:9-11 NRSV)

> This is my prayer: that your love might become even more and more rich with knowledge and all kinds of insight. I pray this so that you will be able to decide what really matters and so you will be sincere and blameless on the day of Christ. I pray that you will then be filled with the fruit of righteousness, which comes from Jesus Christ, in order to give glory and praise to God.
> (Philippians 1:9-11 CEB)

Special Preparation

- Ask participants to bring either a notebook or an electronic means of journaling, such as a tablet. Provide writing paper and pens for those who may need them. Also have Bibles available for those who do not bring one.
- Invite participants to read Chapter 3 in advance of the session and remind them to bring their journals with them.
- Make copies of Handout 3: A Basic Tool of Discernment for the group (see page 58 for a preview; for a printable PDF, see Abingdonpress.com/WhatAreWeFightingFor).
- Have available large sheets of blank paper (newsprint) or construction paper and colored markers for group activity.
- As leader, go over the session in advance and select or adapt the activities you think will work best for your group in the time allotted. Consider your own responses to questions you will pose to the group.
- Make nametags available if desired.

Getting Started

Welcome and Opening Prayer (3 minutes)

As participants arrive, welcome them to the study and invite them to make use of one of the available Bibles, if they did not bring one. Offer the following prayer, pray one of your own, or invite a group member to pray.

God of wisdom and discernment, teach us to link our passion with belief, our belief with action, and our action with you. Amen.

Connecting the Dots

Video (15 minutes)

Play the video for Session 3. This segment acknowledges that there are ups and downs, twists and turns in our lives that can cause us to become frustrated and lose focus, and we are encouraged to sift out the nonessentials so that what remains is what matters most. This process can be challenging and requires courage, vision, discipline, and the help of others. It involves not only searching within but also actively listening to others and valuing their opinions; understanding the context of what's happening around us; searching the Scriptures and history for examples of how God has been at work; and praying that God's Spirit might bring proper perspective.

Choose from the following for a brief discussion:

- How can the past hinder our discernment of what matters most? When have biases or preconceived notions prevented you from discerning God's plan? Why is it dangerous to rely upon assumptions?

- How do introspection, active listening, study of the Scriptures and history, and prayer help us sift out the nonessentials and discern what matters most? What else do you believe is important to the process?

Biblical Foundation (5 minutes)

The author defines *discernment* as "the ability to recognize or determine something that is unique or distinct." He goes on to state his belief that God longs for us to develop a discerning spirit—"the ability not only to distinguish between right and wrong but also to determine those things that are worth fighting for in the midst of the complexities of our world."

Read aloud the biblical passage for this session, Philippians 1:9-11, which is part of Paul's prayer for the church at Philippi. Invite group members to briefly share how this passage connects with the author's statements about the urgent need for discernment in our congregations.

Book Study (20 minutes)

Invite volunteers to *briefly* share highlights from their exercises on healthy relationship skills during the week (Handout 2: The Soil of Healthy Relationships). *Make notes on newsprint and save them for a summary activity in your last group session.*

Point out that healthy relationships are the soil in which our tree of faith is planted, and our practice of the spiritual discipline of discernment is the nourishment for our tree's growth. Explore the content of Chapter 3 together with the following exercises:

Five Guidelines

Remind the participants of the five guidelines for learning and practicing discernment: don't wait; look back to learn; seize the opportunity before you; connect the dots; sift out nonessentials. Spend five minutes discussing how these guidelines shape our practice of spiritual discernment and where you see each guideline expressed in your faith community. Make notes on newsprint or a whiteboard.

Our Church Life

Divide into small groups of four or five. Ask each group to choose a program or ministry of the congregation in the area of worship, mission, education, or leadership and spend ten minutes exploring the ways it fits the guidelines for discernment using the following questions (write them on newsprint or a whiteboard):

- How does this ministry or program help the congregation live out the beliefs of the congregation?
- How does this ministry or program reflect and teach the way of Jesus?

Come back together as a full group and spend five minutes briefly sharing insights from the small groups. *Make notes on newsprint to be saved for a summary activity in your last group session.*

For Deeper Discernment (Additional 30 minutes— Extended Format Only)

The author offers a basic process for discernment in linking passion with belief, belief with action, and action with God. Through growing awareness of our deepest passions, we have the potential to discern God's will for our lives.

Ask each person to name a passion in his or her life (for example, children, work, social justice, community need). Post the following questions on newsprint or a whiteboard and invite individuals to reflect on and journal about them:

- Link passion with belief: in what ways does your passion reflect or relate to your beliefs about life, about God?

- Link belief with action: how do you live out, or take action on, your passion?
- Link action with God: in what ways does your passionate action imitate the life of Jesus? How does it influence or change your relationship with God? with others? with yourself?

Allow about 10 minutes for journaling; then invite persons to share their responses in pairs. Give the pairs about 10 minutes to share. Remind them that as each person shares, the task of the listener is to attend to and receive the story in prayerful silence.

Invite the group together to share new insights and understandings about the relationship between our deepest passions and our discernment of God's will.

The Way Forward

Practical Exercises and Reflections for the Week (5 minutes)

Exercises in this section build on one another as the sessions progress, much as a tree grows from the roots in the soil through the trunk, branches, and leaves. The practical exercises for this session deal with nourishment for our tree of faith: our individual and corporate practice of spiritual discernment.

As a group, read through the final paragraphs of Chapter 3, beginning with, "Discerning what matters most requires sifting through all of the feelings, passions, ideas, beliefs, experiences, and actions that are brought to the table."

Distribute copies of Handout 3: A Basic Tool of Discernment (see page 58 for a preview; for a printable PDF, see Abingdonpress .com/WhatAreWeFightingFor). Instruct group members to post the handout somewhere they will see it daily, using it as a springboard for reflection and action in the coming week. Invite participants to explore the question through the week, filling the blanks with various programs, ministries, beliefs, and values, and to record their responses in their journals. (You might consider choosing three or four options for everyone to explore, so that you have common themes to discuss at the next session.) Tell participants to be sure to bring their journals with them next time, when they will have the opportunity to share highlights with the group.

Closing Prayer (2 minutes)

Come Holy Spirit. Help us to feel your presence as we seek to discern—to understand—what is essential in our love of you, our neighbors, and ourselves. Amen.

Session 4

FILLING IN THE BLANK WITH THE ESSENTIALS

Planning the Session

Session Goals

As a result of conversations and activities connected with this session, group members should begin to:

- Explore four essentials of faith: grace, relationships, joy, and hope.
- Learn to express deeply held beliefs with love and understanding.
- Engage in the spiritual practice of discernment with confidence, letting God "inspire" us rather than us trying to "inspire" God.

Biblical Foundation

"Just so, I tell you, there will be more joy in heaven over one sinner who repents than over ninety-nine righteous persons who need no repentance." (Luke 15:7 NRSV)

"In the same way, I tell you, there will be more joy in heaven over one sinner who changes both heart and life than over ninety-nine righteous people who have no need to change their hearts and lives." (Luke 15:7 CEB)

Special Preparation

- Ask participants to bring either a notebook or an electronic means of journaling, such as a tablet. Provide writing paper and pens for those who may need them. Also have Bibles available for those who do not bring one.
- Invite participants to read Chapter 4 in advance of the session and remind them to bring their journals with them.
- Have available large sheets of blank paper (newsprint) or construction paper and colored markers for group activity.
- Make three copies of Handout 4-A: Church Conflict Roleplay and copies for the group of Handout 4-B: Other Essentials (see pages 59 and 60 for previews; for printable PDFs, see Abingdonpress.com/WhatAreWeFightingFor).
- As leader, you'll want to go over the session in advance and select or adapt the activities you think will work best for your group in the time allotted. Consider your own responses to questions you will pose to the group.
- Make nametags available if desired.

Getting Started

Welcome and Opening Prayer (3 minutes)

As participants arrive, welcome them to the study and invite them to make use of one of the available Bibles, if they did not bring one. Offer the following prayer, pray one of your own, or invite a group member to pray. For this session, you might consider singing together "Fill My Cup, Lord" as your opening and closing prayer (#641 in *The United Methodist Hymnal*).

Fill us with your love, O God. Help us to see, to hear, to feel, and to offer your grace in all that we share this day. Amen.

Connecting the Dots

Video (15 minutes)

Play the video for Session 4. In this segment we learn that prayer can easily be a setup for failure if we dictate to God exactly what we think we need, because it may not be what we need after all. We are encouraged instead to pray for the feelings we would have if God answered our prayers and to leave the specifics up to God—a posture of faith that opens us up to the freshness of the unexpected and the surprise of the unknown. We also review four essentials that are critical in our journey to discover what matters most.

Choose from the following for a brief discussion:

- What can keep us from trusting God to fill in the blanks and meet our deepest longings? How can we open ourselves to the surprises God has in store for us and our churches?
- Do you have the faith and courage to place your feelings in the hands of a loving God? How might the prayer technique suggested in the video be a freeing exercise for you?
- As a church body, how can we put ourselves into the hands of God, trusting God to inform and bless our longings? How willing, able, and ready are we to receive the directions that God has for us?

- In what ways are grace, joy, relationships, and hope foundational essentials for our lives and our churches? How can being too specific about what these essentials look like create problems?

Biblical Foundation (5 minutes)

Invite volunteers to read Luke 15, the stories of the lost sheep, lost coin, and lost son. As the passage is read, invite participants to reflect on the author's statement that "joy is God's eternal desire and basic declaration."

Book Study (20 minutes)

Invite volunteers to *briefly* share highlights of the essentials they identified by "filling in the blank" through the week (Handout 3: A Basic Tool of Discernment). Note similarities among the lists offered and compare them with the author's list of essentials from Chapter 4: grace, relationships, joy, and hope. *Make notes on newsprint and save them for a summary activity in your last group session.*

You may choose to spend 10 minutes on this exercise and another 10 minutes on the roleplay below (Choices). Or, if you prefer to have more time to discuss the essentials, you may choose to skip the roleplay.

Choices

In this chapter's section on relationships, the author shares several scenarios to highlight the value of relationships and the importance of treating others as Jesus did—particularly when there is disagreement or conflict. Use this roleplay exercise to invite participants to explore what this might look like in a church setting.

Invite three volunteers to participate in a scenario roleplay. Distribute Handout 4-A: Church Conflict Roleplay to each of the volunteers (see page 59 for a preview; for a printable PDF, see Abingdonpress.com/WhatAreWeFightingFor). As they act out their parts, invite the rest of the group to note the way the "actors" interact and the choices they make in their responses to one another.

When the roleplay reaches a natural conclusion, invite the "actors" and the rest of the group to reflect on the experience. Discuss:

- What worked well?
- What different choices would have helped the conversation move more smoothly?
- For the "actors," what did the experience feel like?
- What is required for difficult conversations to be filled with the grace and kindness that Jesus demonstrated?

For Deeper Discernment (Additional 30 minutes— Extended Format Only)

Invite participants to review the author's section on *hope* and then reflect on and record their responses to the following questions:

- What are your hopes for your life?
- What are the dilemmas and obstacles you (or the congregation) need to work through to realize these hopes? What are the risks?

Give about ten minutes for this review and reflection time. Invite participants, in pairs, to share their personal hopes.

Divide into small groups of three or four. Invite each group to name their hopes for the congregation, noting again dilemmas, obstacles, and risks. Ask the groups to record their responses on newsprint and choose a reporter. When the groups have completed their work, invite the reporter from each group to post the newsprint and share the group's findings. *Be sure to save the newsprint notes for a summary activity in your last group session.*

Note areas of commonality among the group responses. Discuss the benefit of defining essentials through community discernment in identifying and realizing hopes.

The Way Forward

Practical Exercises and Reflections for the Week (5 minutes)

Exercises in this section build on one another as the sessions progress, much as a tree grows from the roots in the soil through the trunk, branches, and leaves. In this session, we begin to see the trunk of the tree grow straight and tall—having healthy roots and being planted in good soil and nourished by the food of our shared spiritual practices. We are filling in the blank, defining the essentials of our faith, and growing together to reach the sun.

The author writes that when working with churches, he often puts himself in the shoes of a potential visitor and creates a mental checklist of things that would keep him from returning for another service. Invite participants to plan to tour the church one Sunday morning with the eyes of a visitor. They might want to do this in teams, or invite a friend who is not a church member to join them, sharing observations as they go. Encourage them to write down the following questions to ask themselves when they take the tour (post them on newsprint or a whiteboard):

- What witness do the building and grounds offer of Christ's love?
- Where are grace, joy, healthy relationships, and hope evident in the life of the church?
- If you were attending for the first time, would you return?

- Now distribute copies of Handout 4-B: Other Essentials (see page 60 for a preview; for a printable PDF, see Abingdonpress.com/WhatAreWeFightingFor). (If time permits, you might want to read aloud the final section of the chapter, Other Essentials.) Instruct participants to post the handout somewhere they will see it daily, using it as a springboard for reflection and action in the coming week. Invite them to review their personal hopes, hopes for the church, and their growing list of essentials in light of the author's questions on the handout, and to record their thoughts in their journals. Tell participants to be sure to bring their journals with them next time, when they will have the opportunity to share highlights with the group.

Closing Prayer (2 minutes)

God of grace, joy, and hope, God of loving relationship, walk with us as we see with new eyes, hear with new ears, as we build our lives on the essentials of faith. Amen.

Session 5

PADDLING IN THE SAME CANOE

Planning the Session

Session Goals

As a result of conversations and activities connected with this session, group members should begin to:

- Understand the application of unity, liberty, and charity in naming and living essentials.
- Explore the difference between conformity and embracing diversity.
- Learn the value of holy conferencing.

Biblical Foundation

> Now there are varieties of gifts, but the same Spirit; and there are varieties of services, but the same Lord; and there are varieties of activities, but it is the same God who activates all of them in everyone. To each is given the manifestation of the Spirit for the common good. . . . All these are activated by one and the same Spirit, who allots to each one individually just as the Spirit chooses.
>
> For just as the body is one and has many members, and all the members of the body, though many, are one body, so it is with Christ. For in the one Spirit we were all baptized into one body—Jews or Greeks, slaves or free—and we were all made to drink of one Spirit.
>
> (1 Corinthians 12:4-7, 11-13 NRSV)

> There are different spiritual gifts but the same Spirit; and there are different ministries and the same Lord; and there are different activities but the same God who produces all of them in everyone. A demonstration of the Spirit is given to each person for the common good. . . . All these things are produced by the one and same Spirit who gives what he wants to each person.
>
> Christ is just like the human body—a body is a unit and has many parts; and all the parts of the body are one body, even though there are many. We were all baptized by one Spirit into one body, whether Jew or Greek, or slave or free, and we all were given one Spirit to drink.
>
> (1 Corinthians 12:4-7, 11-13 CEB)

Special Preparation

- Ask participants to bring either a notebook or an electronic means of journaling, such as a tablet. Provide writing paper and pens for those who may need them. Also have Bibles available for those who do not bring one.
- Invite participants to read Chapter 5 in advance of the session and remind them to bring their journals with them.

- Have available large sheets of blank paper (newsprint) or construction paper and colored markers for group activity.
- Post on newsprint or a whiteboard 1 Corinthians 12:4-7, 11-13.
- Make copies of Handout 5: Holy Conferencing for the group (see page 61 for a preview; for a printable PDF, see Abingdonpress.com/WhatAreWeFightingFor).
- As leader, you'll want to go over the session in advance and select or adapt the activities you think will work best for your group in the time allotted. Consider your own responses to questions you will pose to the group.
- Make nametags available if desired.

Getting Started

Welcome and Opening Prayer (3 minutes)

As participants arrive, welcome them to the study and invite them to make use of one of the available Bibles, if they did not bring one. Offer the following prayer, pray one of your own, or invite a group member to pray.

As the body of Christ, O Lord, help us learn to embrace our diversity and live in the oneness of your love. Amen.

Connecting the Dots

Video (15 minutes)

Play the video for Session 5. In this segment we are reminded that we are stronger together than we are by ourselves. There is great power when we choose to paddle in the same canoe. We are encouraged to let go of the idea that there is one right way to live out our faith and embrace the freedom that comes when we identify the things we share in common while appreciating the diversity of thought and practice in others who have been created by the same wonderful and loving God.

Choose from the following for a brief discussion:

- How can we actively search—as individual churches and as a denomination—for the things we share in common? How can this common focus and drive help us see the good in one another and appreciate our differences?
- Why is it critical for us to be free to live out our faith using our different gifts and talents in the variety of contexts in which we live and minister?
- How can we foster an environment that allows and encourages diversity in the expression of our essential beliefs?

Biblical Foundation (5 minutes)

Direct the group members' attention to 1 Corinthians 12:4-7, 11-13, which you posted on newsprint or a whiteboard. (Note that those verses that list individual gifts of the Spirit are intentionally excluded so that the conversation can focus on the unity of the Spirit in the body of Christ.) Before reading the verses aloud, have the group members count off from one to three, with each person saying a number in turn until everyone has a number. Then give these instructions:

As I read the passage aloud, I want all number one's to listen for words or phrases that relate to unity, all number two's to listen for words or phrases that relate to freedom (our freedom and God's freedom), and all number three's to listen for words or phrases that relate to love.

Invite the three groups to briefly share some of the words and phrases that were meaningful for them in relation to unity, freedom, and love.

Book Study (20 minutes)

Invite volunteers to *briefly* share highlights of the hopes and essentials they listed during the week (Handout 4-B: Other Essentials). *Make notes on newsprint and save them for a summary activity in your last group session.* Note the similarities and differences among the essentials named. Point out the importance of unity when there are differences of opinion around what matters most or how we are to live out those priorities as individuals and as the church.

Chapter 5 explores in detail a saying that can help to guide the life of faith in healthy and vital communities: "In essentials, unity; in nonessentials, liberty; in all things, love." Share with the group this excerpt from the author's introduction to the chapter, which sets the stage for the following exercise:

> What if, as you identify the things that provide the foundation for your church's ministry, the discussion leads to a fork in the road or a difference of opinion around what matters most or how we are to live out those priorities in our public witness—both as a church and as individuals? This is the overarching question we will explore in this chapter as we remind ourselves how important it is not only to paddle in the same canoe but also to pull together in a synchronized strategy that clearly demonstrates our commitment to what matters most.

Defining Essentials through Holy Conferencing

Have the group members divide into three groups according to their numbers from earlier. Assign each group one example considered in the chapter: 1) The Bible and Biblical Interpretation,

2) Theological Beliefs, 3) Compassion for Others (beginning on page 106). Ask each group to review the assigned section in the chapter and form together a statement that expresses the essential nature of this example as they understand it. Assure them that they need not be concerned about producing a fully developed statement; there will not be time. The importance of the exercise is how they work through differences of opinion. Before they begin, remind them of the chapter's lesson that "people who think differently are not necessarily wrong."

Before the groups begin, share these three fundamental questions for consensus making (write them on newsprint or a whiteboard):

Do you agree?

Do you disagree but are willing to stand aside so the idea can move forward?

Do you disagree and are unwilling to move forward?

Give the groups five to seven minutes to work together, then call them together to share their experiences. Remember to focus on the process, not the actual statements they may or may not have produced. Ask each group to share in response to the following questions:

- Did they all agree on the essential nature of the assigned area?
- If they disagreed, were they able to express that calmly and reasonably?
- How did they deal with feelings of anger or frustration that may have emerged?
- What did they learn from the experience?

For Deeper Discernment (Additional 30 minutes— Extended Format Only)

Share with the group this quotation from *The United Methodist Book of Discipline*: "The local church provides the most significant arena through which disciple-making occurs" (*The United Methodist Book of Discipline* [Nashville: The United Methodist Publishing House, 2012], ¶201, 143). This can happen only when we learn how to work together in harmony.

Divide into the same three groups once again and ask each group to design a new ministry in the area of mission, social justice, education, or worship. Distribute or make available newsprint and markers for the groups to record their work. *Be sure to save the newsprint notes for a summary activity in your last group session.*

Instruct them to employ the discernment process learned in Chapter 3 and to find consensus on the essentials of faith that will undergird their ministry. Remind them of the three questions related to consensus making. They will need to use all the skills they have learned in previous sessions to guide their work. Again, the process employed is the focus here, not the outcome. (Although it's possible that the outcome may bear fruit for a future ministry.)

Give the small groups fifteen to twenty minutes to work. Invite the groups back together and ask each group to share the process they followed, any outcome they have to report, and the lessons of the experience itself.

The Way Forward

Practical Exercises and Reflections for the Week (5 minutes)

Exercises in this section build on one another as the sessions progress, much as a tree grows from the roots in the soil through the trunk, branches, and leaves. Point out that the practical exercises for this session invite us to begin to "branch out," to use the skills and lessons we have been learning in living out our faith in the world. Each branch is unique and beautiful in its own way if it grows from the strong trunk and roots, which are planted in good soil and nourished by healthy relationships and the discernment of God's will.

Distribute copies of Handout 5: Holy Conferencing (see page 61 for a preview; for a printable PDF, see Abingdonpress.com/ WhatAreWeFightingFor). Instruct participants to post the handout somewhere they will see it daily, reflecting on the guidelines for holy conferencing throughout the week. Invite each person to engage in holy conferencing with another person sometime during the week (either from the group or beyond the group) using the handout as a guide. Encourage them to record their experiences in their journals.

Tell participants that it is especially important for them to bring their journals with them to the last session, when you will document together both the essentials and nonessentials you have determined through this process of discernment. Encourage them to spend time this week reviewing their notes and considering what essentials have risen to the top, as well as how those essentials might be lived out in various ministries.

Closing Prayer (2 minutes)

God of essentials, of love and freedom and grace, of joy and hope and relationships, help us to take the lessons of this time together into the world as we seek to live as faithful disciples of Jesus the Christ. Amen.

Session 6

FINISHING WITH LOVE

Planning the Session

Session Goals

As a result of conversations and activities connected with this session, group members should begin to:

- Learn about the vertical and horizontal nature of Christian love.
- Explore the influence of love on the choices we make in our lives and in our congregation.
- Understand the significance of Wesley's General Rules and their application in our lives of faith.
- Document "what matters most" and visualize how these essentials can be lived out through various ministries.

Biblical Foundation

"Teacher, which commandment in the law is the greatest?" [Jesus replied], "'You shall love the Lord your God with all your heart, and with all your soul, and with all your mind.' This is the greatest and first commandment. And a second is like it: 'You shall love your neighbor as yourself.'" (Matthew 22:36-39 NRSV)

"Teacher, what is the greatest commandment in the Law?"
[Jesus] replied, "You must love the Lord your God with all your heart, with all your being, and with all your mind. This is the first and greatest commandment. And the second is like it: You must love your neighbor as you love yourself." (Matthew 22:36-39 CEB)

Special Preparation

- Ask participants to bring either a notebook or an electronic means of journaling, such as a tablet. Provide writing paper and pens for those who may need them. Also have Bibles available for those who do not bring one.
- Invite participants to read Chapter 6 in advance of the session and remind them of the importance of bringing their journals with them for a summary activity.
- Collect all of the newsprint notes you have been saving throughout the study and bring them to your last group session for a summary activity.
- Make copies for the group of Handout 6-A: The Big Picture: A Summary Activity, and Handout 6-B: Behavioral Covenant (see pages 62 and 63 for previews; for printable PDFs, see Abingdonpress.com/WhatAreWeFightingFor).
- As leader, you'll want to go over the session in advance and select or adapt the activities you think will work best for your group in the time allotted. Consider your own responses to questions you will pose to the group.
- Make nametags available if desired.

Getting Started

Welcome and Opening Prayer (3 minutes)

As participants arrive, welcome them to the study and invite them to make use of one of the available Bibles, if they did not bring one. Offer the following prayer, pray one of your own, or invite a group member to pray.

Gracious and loving God, as our study draws to a close, fill us with your power and presence, so that all that we learn here might become all that we are in the world. We ask this in Jesus' name. Amen.

Connecting the Dots

Video (15 minutes)

Play the video for Session 6. This final segment reminds us that in a world of controversy, chaos, and discord, we are called to demonstrate a better way—the way of love. Our God loves us with a love that will not let us go, and we are called to love one another in just the same way. Though we cannot be a community of Polyanna denials of reality, we can and should be a community where disagreement is surrounded and informed by love. In fact, our greatest public witness is our demonstration of how deeply we love God and, as a result, how much we love one another in spite of our differences.

Choose from the following for a brief discussion:

- How do our internal fights and disagreements damage our public witness as a church?
- How would our lives and our churches be changed if we were to see every challenge as a God-given opportunity to

demonstrate for a hurting and broken world that there is a better way—the way of love? Why is love a choice we must make daily?

• What can we do to shift our focus and energies from the things that are nonessential, which often divide us, to the things that matter most, which can unite us?

Biblical Foundation (5 minutes)

Read aloud Matthew 22:36-39. Then read to the group this quotation from the book (pp. 122-123):

> We express this love that is within us in two directions. The first direction our love takes is vertical, toward God. At the center of our love for God is our belief that God is an active part of our engagement in the world. We demonstrate our love for God most clearly in our devotion to worship, where we lift our praise and adoration to the one who created us, who loves us, and who sustains us by the gift of grace.
>
> The second direction our love takes is horizontal, toward all of God's creation. We demonstrate the depth of our belief in God as creator in the way we care for all that God has created, including our neighbor. The connection between faith and ministries of love is what creates the depth of our spirituality and the breadth of our Christian discipleship.*

Invite group members to briefly share how the passage and excerpt reflect or challenge their understanding of *love*.

Book Study (20 minutes)

Invite a couple of volunteers to *briefly* share highlights of their holy conferencing with another person during the week (Handout 5: Holy Conferencing). (Limit to 2-3 minutes.)

---

* Author paraphrase; see *The Book of Discipline of The United Methodist Church 2012* (Nashville: The United Methodist Publishing House, 2012), 52.

Spend 2-3 minutes highlighting the two strategies in Chapter 6. Remind participants that the author states emphatically that "it is a *daily decision* to love God and love others" (p. 127, emphasis added); he also writes:

> The most successful worship experiences are those that have a specific, desired outcome.... What would it look like if love were the desired outcome not only each time we gather for worship but also for every program, activity, and meeting that takes place in our congregations? That might be the source of transformation and renewal we have been looking for all along—all because of an intentional decision to make love the primary agenda for the life of our church. (pp. 128-129)

Challenge participants to make a commitment to these two strategies (if you like, you may write them in advance on newsprint or a whiteboard):

1. Decide daily to love God and love others.
2. Strive for love to be the desired outcome for everything our church does.

The Big Picture: A Summary Activity

In advance of the session, collect the newsprint notes you have saved throughout the study and post them in the room where all can see them. Distribute copies of Handout 6-A: The Big Picture, and work together as a group to fill in the blanks on the roots and trunk with those things you believe are the essentials for the life and witness of your church. Invite participants to review the newsprint notes and their own journal entries as you discuss and identify the things that have risen to the top of your collective discernment. (Allow 5 minutes.)

Next, work on filling in the blanks on the branches with some of the nonessentials—those things that give expression to the essentials. (Allow 5 minutes.)

Conclude by discussing how the essentials you have identified might be lived out in various ministries. (Allow 5 minutes.)

If you would like to devote more time to this exercise, plan a time when you can come back together to complete your discussion and documentation. Try to choose a time when everyone can be present, if possible. You might consider meeting in someone's home and/or sharing a meal or celebratory activity afterward. Or, if you are having an extended session, you might elect to continue this summary activity in lieu of "For Deeper Discernment" below. Choose whichever option is best for your group.

For Deeper Discernment (Additional 30 minutes—Extended Format Only)

The author lifts up John Wesley's General Rules for the Methodist Societies (see p. 123; see also *The Book of Discipline,* ¶102, p. 52). Distribute copies of Handout 6-B: Behavioral Covenant (see page 63; for a printable PDF, see Abingdonpress.com/leaderguides).

Invite the group to form a covenant of behavior that incorporates the lessons learned throughout these sessions and their growing understanding of love. Begin with prayer, silent or spoken. As you pose the questions related to each of the three rules in order, list group responses on newsprint or a whiteboard and invite participants to list them on the back of their handout as well.

After the exercise, ask the group if they are willing to abide by the provisions of this covenant. Take some time to allow for challenges and questions, observing the guidelines for holy conferencing. End the conversation with prayer and gratitude for the shared work.

The Way Forward

Practical Exercises and Reflections for the Week (5 minutes)

Exercises in this section have been building on one another as the sessions progress, much as a tree grows from the roots in the soil through the trunk, branches, and leaves. The practical exercise for this final session deals with the fruit we produce and share: the love that grows through our shared life of faithful discipleship.

Share this quotation from the book:

> Finishing with love is coming to the realization that the ending point is also the starting line. Love is the source of our being, the fuel for the journey, and the goal for which we live. God has reached into the incubator of life and touched us with the warmth of love. Will we have the courage to do the same "in all things"? (p. 130)

If you have an extended session and have formed a behavioral covenant together, invite participants to state their commitment to abide by its provisions and to help one another do so. Otherwise, invite participants to state their commitment to help one another grow in love, to have the courage to bring love into each relationship and every meeting, and to help one another along the way—to fight for a community of faith filled with grace, joy, healthy relationships, and hope.

Close with this quotation from the epilogue:

> I believe God wants every one of us and each of our churches to play our part in the big story of making and nurturing disciples on the journey. This book has been an attempt to remind us that now is the time to refocus our attention on the things that Jesus told us we should be and do. We will never find complete agreement on any issue, but we can find our focus when we discover God's amazing love for us and the limitless possibilities we have to share that love with others.

Closing Prayer (2 minutes)

God of eternal love, fill us with your power as we leave this place, so that all we have shared and learned here helps us to be more faithful disciples. As your church in and for the world, we pray in the name of Jesus the Christ. Amen.

Handout 1

THE ROOTS OF OUR FAITH

Post this handout somewhere you will see it daily and use it as a springboard for reflection and action in the coming week.

Reflect and act on these five "I" words throughout the week as you encounter conversations and activities in your personal life and in the life of your church. Or you may prefer to focus on a different word each day. Record your thoughts and experiences in your journal.

1. Inspiration

Reflect: How do you draw on spiritual strength in encounters with others—especially difficult people or situations? How well does your church do this?
Act: Pray that God might inspire you this week and use you to be an inspiration for others, and then watch for an opportunity.

2. Integration

Reflect: How are spiritual disciplines or practices a part of your daily walk? How does this enable you to respond to others in love and enter into conversations about faith? How does your church encourage and incorporate spiritual practices?
Act: Consider one opportunity this week where you can integrate your faith into practice. This may be a witness you might provide, a habit you need to address, or an action you can perform.

3. Isolation

Reflect: When you experience isolation, what do you do to reach out and overcome it? What opportunities exist to create or deepen relationships between your church and the community?
Act: Identify and reach out to one person you do not know well or do not agree with on some issue. Make a phone call, write a note, send an e-mail, or extend an invitation for coffee. Let the person know of your desire to know him or her better.

4. Independence

Reflect: How is your relationship with God? How does your daily life demonstrate your reliance upon God?
Act: Spend time this week praying that you might be blessed with a greater understanding of what it means to be dependent on God's guidance and direction.

5. Invitation

Reflect: When was the last time you shared your story of faith with someone? In what ways can your church invite others to share in the story of God's love in Christ?
Act: Pray that God might reveal to you an opportunity to invite someone to your church. Be actively looking for that opportunity, and pray for the courage to invite someone to join you this week.

For a printable PDF, see Abingdonpress.com/WhatAreWeFightingFor.

Handout 2

THE SOIL OF RELATIONSHIPS

Post this handout somewhere you will see it daily and use it as a springboard for reflection and action in the coming week.

Seek opportunities this week to listen with love and learn from others as you implement three reminders of healthy relationship skills. Record your thoughts and experiences in your journal.

1. Loosen up.

In conversations or meetings with difficult people, intentionally focus on breathing deeply and making space for the possibility of finding common ground.

2. Collaborate.

Identify a project—at home, work, or church—that involves other people. Intentionally seek help from others in making decisions about the project.

3. Open to the possibility of change.

Read an article or seek a conversation with someone whose viewpoint differs from yours. Practice active listening and note new ideas that emerge.

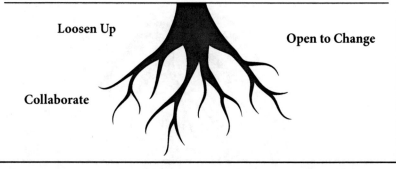

Loosen Up

Open to Change

Collaborate

For a printable PDF, see Abingdonpress.com/WhatAreWeFightingFor.

Handout 3

A BASIC TOOL OF DISCERNMENT

Post this handout somewhere you will see it daily and use it as a springboard for reflection and action in the coming week.

Explore the question below throughout the week, filling in the blank with various programs, ministries, beliefs, and values. Reflect on whether each is essential or nonessential. Record your thoughts in your journal.

If _____ went away, could you still have a church?

Essential vs. Nonessential

Essential: Absolutely necessary for the life and growth of the body of Christ. Gets to the very core of who we are and what we cannot lose in the expression of our church.

Nonessential: Not required for the life and growth of the body of Christ. Important, but not what matters most.

For a printable PDF, see Abingdonpress.com/WhatAreWeFightingFor.

Handout 4-A

A CHURCH CONFLICT ROLEPLAY

Background

A new pastor has made a number of changes at the church, including rearranging furniture and revamping the order of worship and church website. When the pastor was appointed, he or she was assured that the congregation wanted to grow and would support new ideas. Now the pastor is coming to a meeting to share a proposal to launch a new praise service and move the traditional service from 11:00 a.m. to 9:00 a.m. to accommodate the new service. As the meeting begins, each person demands to "have their say" first. The pastor launches into the proposal, but each person interrupts along the way.

Role Descriptions

Person 1

This is a long-time member whose family helped to grow the church in its early days. The mother played organ in the church for years, but the new pastor wants to have the instrument removed from the sanctuary. This person constantly holds the former pastor up as a role model and compares the current pastor, always unfavorably. He or she says at every meeting, "I don't see what's wrong with the way things are!"

Person 2

This person is fed up with all the changes and disruptions caused by the new pastor. One of the biggest financial givers in the congregation, he or she is attending the meeting to deliver the message: "If there are any more changes, I will withhold giving until things are returned to the way they were before." He or she has no interest in hearing a proposal for anything else new and is ready to write the district superintendent to request a change of pastor.

Pastor

The pastor is unaware of the anxiety and unhappiness in the congregation and thinks he or she is doing exactly what the congregation asks and expects. He or she is passionate and excited about the new service and bursting with ideas for ways the church can change and improve. The pastor dismisses disagreement or argument as people simply are not yet understanding how good the ideas are.

Scenario adapted from "Healthy Boundaries Training" by Dan and Barbara Dick, 2010. Used by permission.

For a printable PDF, see Abingdonpress.com/WhatAreWeFightingFor.

Handout 4-B

OTHER ESSENTIALS

Post this handout somewhere you will see it daily and use it as a springboard for reflection and action in the coming week.

Reflect on the questions below throughout the week. Consider whether your hopes and the "essentials" that you believe matter most are driven by the mission and passion of Jesus—not by a personal agenda or passion. Record your thoughts in your journal.

- Does grace matter in what we do and how we do it?

- Do relationships make a difference in the way that we proclaim God's love?

- Is joy evident in our ongoing work?

- Do we hope for a better day than the one we are currently experiencing?

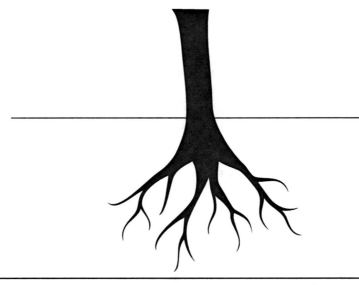

For a printable PDF, see Abingdonpress.com/WhatAreWeFightingFor.

Handout 5

HOLY CONFERENCING

Guidelines:

1. Every person is a child of God.
2. Listen before speaking.
3. Strive to understand from another's point of view.
4. Strive to reflect accurately the views of others.
5. Disagree without being disagreeable.
6. Speak about issues; do not defame people.
7. Pray, in silence or aloud, before decisions.
8. Let prayer interrupt your busy-ness.[1]

Instructions:

1. Begin by reading this prayer aloud together:

   A Covenant Prayer in the Wesleyan Tradition
   I am no longer my own, but thine.
   Put me to what thou wilt, rank me with whom thou wilt.
   Put me to doing, put me to suffering.
   Let me be employed by thee or laid aside for thee,
   exalted for thee or brought low by thee.
   Let me have all things, let me have nothing.
   I freely and heartily yield all things
   to thy pleasure and disposal.
   And now, O glorious and blessed God,
   Father, Son, and Holy Spirit,
   thou art mine, and I am thine. So be it.
   And the covenant which I have made on earth,
   let it be ratified in heaven. Amen.[2]

2. After you have prayed, be in silence together for a moment or two.
3. Together, consider and discuss this question, observing the eight guidelines for holy conferencing: "What is essential for the church to be a vital witness to the love of Christ in the world?" It is not necessary that you come to agreement; the idea is to observe the eight guidelines for holy conferencing as you share with one another.
4. End your conversation by reading the covenant prayer again with gratitude for the opportunity to share.

1. Bishop Sally Dyck, "Eight Principles of Holy Conferencing: A Study Guide for Churches and Groups," https://www .minnesotaumc.org/assets/uploads/documents/Holy_Conferencing_Study_Guide_2012.pdf (Minneapolis: 2012), 3–14.

2. *The United Methodist Hymnal* (Nashville: The United Methodist Publishing House, 1989), 607.

For a printable PDF, see Abingdonpress.com/WhatAreWeFightingFor.

Handout 6-A

THE BIG PICTURE

(A Summary Activity)

Discuss and identify with your group the essentials that have risen to the top of your collective discernment—those things that matter most to the life and witness of your church. Write them in the roots and trunk of the tree.

Next, identify some of the nonessentials that have become clear during the discernment process—those things that give expression to the essentials—and write these in the branches.

Finally, spend time visualizing together how the essentials you have identified might be lived out in various ministries.

NONESSENTIALS

_____   _____

_____   _____

_____   _____

ESSENTIALS

_____   _____

_____   _____

ESSENTIALS

_____   _____

_____   _____

For a printable PDF, see Abingdonpress.com/WhatAreWeFightingFor.

Handout 6-B

BEHAVIORAL COVENANT

John Wesley's general rules were clear and simple:

> It is therefore expected of all who continue therein that they should continue to evidence their desire for salvation,
> First: By doing no harm, by avoiding evil of every kind...
> Secondly: By...doing good of every possible sort, and, as far as possible, to all...
> Thirdly: By attending upon all the ordinances of God.[1]

These three general rules offer a simple approach to formulating a behavioral covenant for a congregation or other group. Members can respond to the statements and formulate lists. Then follow-up conversations about the lists can help the group members reach consensus on the practices and behaviors that all will observe and engage. The resulting covenant can be signed by everyone who contributed. As the covenant practices become the norm, group members will begin to self-regulate when an unacceptable behavior occurs. The strengthened spiritual environment can have impact beyond the group.

First, Do No Harm

What are the behaviors and actions that "do harm" to healthy relationships? What are the practices and behaviors that we promise *not* to engage in? Items such as gossip and lying are often at the top of this list, and the group should prayerfully consider behaviors that are obstacles to its effectiveness.

Second, Do All the Good You Can

What are the behaviors and actions that "do good to all"? What are the practices and behaviors that we promise to engage in and support? Consider what actions and behaviors will be of specific help in increasing our grace, joy, and hope in mission and ministry.

Third, Attend to All the Ordinances of God

What are the spiritual practices (ordinances)—such as prayer, Scripture reading and reflection, singing, fasting, discernment, holy conferencing—that we believe build a stronger sense of community and fellowship? How will we commit to engage these practices together?

---

1. *The United Methodist Book of Discipline, 2012* (Nashville: The United Methodist Publishing House, 2012), 52.

Adapted from Dan R. Dick, *Congregational Covenant*, 1999. Used by permission.

For a printable PDF, see Abingdonpress.com/WhatAreWeFightingFor.

CPSIA information can be obtained
at www.ICGtesting.com
Printed in the USA
LVOW12s0509060516

486923LV00004B/4/P

9 781501 815072